ASHLEY'S STORY
JUDY BERG

PUBLISHED by PARABLES
Earthly Stories with a Heavenly Meaning

Ashley's Story
Judy Berg

Published By Parables
Febuary, 2020

All Rights Reserved. No part of this book may be reproduced or utilized in any form or by any means, electronic or mechanical, including photocopying, recording, or by any information storage and retrieval system, without permission in writing from the author.

> ISBN 978-1-951497-29-3
> Printed in the United States of America

Readers should be aware that Internet Web sites offered as citations and/or sources for further information may have been changed or disappeared between the time this was written and the time it is read.

Ashley's Story
Judy Berg

PUBLISHED by PARABLES
Earthly Stories with a Heavenly Meaning

Ashley's Story

Every Sunday Gammie Judy prepares a large meal after church. On this particular beautiful fall Sunday, she embellished her dining room with as many stuffed animals, as she could find. She had stuffed cows, pigs, ducks, chickens, a horse and a bear that she decorated the dinning room with. It was going to be a surprise for her granddaughter Ashley, who is spending the day with her grandparents. Ashley, loves all animals. She

Judy Berg

talks about the animals all the time and has such a gift working with them. The kids at school call her the animal whisperer. She loves her nick name!

Gammie Judy stood at the dining room door way with her hands resting on her hips admiring her work of love for her granddaughter. Instinctively Gammie Judy knew that Ashley is going to love this room, as she thought to herself staring at all the food she had prepared, along with

Ashley's Story

all of the stuffed animals. She had cooked a roast with all the trimmings, a fruit basket and Ashley's favorite cake was sitting on the dining room table.

Papa Ron walked up beside Judy, slightly giggling, Oh, dear did you miss anything? Papa Ron teasingly asked with a broad smile as she whirled around on both heels. I don't know, seems like I am missing something, just can't put my finger on it, Judy curiously replied. What about elves

Judy Berg

Papa Ron playfully interjected? Oh, Ron stop it! Sweetie you did a great job, its beautiful and Ashley will love it.

Matter of fact where is Ashley? Has Ashley changed out of her church clothes? I haven't seen Ashley or Poocho, Papa Ron responded, softly rubbing his chin.

Ashley's Story

Chapter 2

Ashley, was reciting The Lord's prayer with Poocho. Poocho was wagging his tail with his tongue out jumping up and down on Ashley as he walked around the stock tank. Stop! Stop! Stop! You are going to make me fall…..Oh look what happened you made me fall in the mud Poocho! Look what

Judy Berg

you made me do Ashley repeated to Poocho, as she is stepping out of the soft mud. I am in trouble now Ashley told herself and Poocho. Ashley fell on her knees and hands, oh no all the while Poocho was licking and jumping all over her. Stop! Stop! Poocho Stop! Ashley, cried out at the top of her lungs. From a distance Ashley heard Gammie Judy calling her. Ashley, Ashley, where are you? Time for lunch. Gammie has a surprise for you. Come on Poocho Ashley excitedly cried

Ashley's Story

out. Instinctively wiping her muddy hands on her pure white Sunday dress. Gammie and Papa have something for me Ashley exclaimed as she quickly ran towards the house. Gammie Judy cuffed her mouth while looking at Ashley wide eyed. Ashley, honey what did you get yourself into? You look a mess. And look at Poocho he has mud everywhere, Gammie Judy exclaimed!

Gammie,Gammie it's not my fault, it was an accident Ashley politely told Gammie, trying to hold back her tears. Ashley added I'm sorry Gammie I promise it will never happen again. Ashley, how may times have you told me that? You are not like the animals that live outside. What am I going to do about you and all these animals? Ashley absolutely no more play time with any animals for a week. Gammie No No they are my only friends! Gammie I have to feed and walk them Ashley said sadly.

Ashley's Story

Chapter 3

Papa Ron curiously walked up to all the commotion slightly smiling at Judy then at Ashley and Poocho. Okay there's only one thing that can make this all go away. Let's start over, Papa Ron replied rubbing his hands together. First, I think it would be best to clean up, then we can talk over lunch. We can start over like nothing ever happened. We can be one big happy family again. How does that sound? Ron you don't make things any better Judy interrupted folding her arms. Well can Ashley and I wash her dress? No No Ron Ashley and I are going to get her cleaned up and you can clean the mud off of Poocho. First Ashley go take a shower and I will wash your dress.

Gathering at the dining room table after everyone is cleaned Ashley exclaimed at how beautiful the table was and

Ashley's Story

loved all the stuff animals Gammie Judy had set around the room. Let's give grace. Thank The Lord for all our blessings, the beautiful stuff animals, the delicious food and of course for the cake Ashley thankfully said. Gammie can I take the baby chickens and my horse Wyoming something to eat? We have enough leftover food to feed all the animals Gammie. Ron, what are we going to do with Ashley? She just loves those animals so much. Well, they are God's creations and we are required to take care of them. You can feed then after your nap. After eating all the wonderful food, it was time for a Sunday afternoon nap. Is Papa going to take a nap too Ashley quietly asked underneath her breath? Yes, we are all going to take a nap. Papa hugged Ashley, gave her a wink as she walked to her bedroom.

Ron I am worried that Ashley will run into the wrong animal, like a snake or worse a bear, Judy whispered as Ashley left

Ashley's Story

the dining room to take her nap.

Ashley poked her head around the corner I love you both! Ashley bellowed then disappeared.

Instinctively Ashley gracefully put all her stuff animals around her as she comfortably laid down for her nap.

Judy Berg

Ashley's Story

Chapter 4

Ashley tells all her animal friends to have a good nap. Ashley, prays for Gammie Judy, Papa Ron and for all her animals. She asked if all her animals could live in her room with her and the stuff animals she would put in the closet. Soon Ashley found herself falling into a deep sleep.

Ashley woke up to find herself lying under her favorite big oak tree. Not believing what she was hearing she began looking around. Ashley found herself consumed with unfamiliar sounds surrounding her. Ashley, quickly surveyed her surroundings with a broad smile on her face. The unfamiliar sounds she heard were animals talking.

About time you woke up girl, we have been waiting all morning for you.

Ashley, what is 8x9+61 Hattie and Speckles asked? Do you have an answer Ashley? She

Ashley's Story

doesn't know Speckles interjected. Yes, I do said Ashley. The answer is 133, see I do know. That makes no sense to me, Speckles has 100 baby chicks a year and she can't add one plus one Wyoming the horse teasingly interrupted, chuckling at the same time. Then Wyoming added, do you know what 2+2 is? Hattie said yes, the answer is 9! No Ashley replied it is 4.

I love chicken wings. I love chicken wings. Molly the cat nonchalantly walked by repeating I love chicken wings. Ashley snickered at Poocho as he stood beside her jumping up and down.

I can't tell Gammie and Papa about the animals talking we are supposed to be taking a nap.

Ashley's Story

Chapter 5

A nap! Child do me a favor, these eight children of mine are driving me crazy. I need a nap! Take them with you so I can get some peace and quiet!!

Hattie the goose is a kid herself Speckles the chicken interjected. Please give her rest Pete the duck interrupted while floating in the stock tank.

Ashley excitingly exclaimed y'all can talk like me? No way!

Judy Berg

The animals looked at her as they continued talking to one another, while going about their routines. Poocho quickly moved behind Ashley looking around with wide eyes.

Wow! Wow! Wow! Poocho, I can't believe what I am seeing and hearing.

Don't listen to Hattie Speckles stated these eight are my kids. Hattie, do you want to buy one Wyoming asked? Speckles spoke up they aren't for sale. Suddenly Ashley busted out

Ashley's Story

snickering and giggling, they are so cute. What are their names? Speckles said I just call them by numbers. 1,2,3,4,5,6,7,8! Time for them to stop eating and take a nap also. Please let me get some rest. You notice they don't pay much attention to me....they hear their mama all day long every day. I need rest. Hattie asked Ashley again do you want one or more? Hattie that isn't funny replied their mama Speckles.

Judy Berg

Ashley turned staring at Wyoming the horse as he gracefully opened the gate letting himself out of his stall. Wyoming, can you talk too, as Ashley ran towards him? Wyoming, I love you Ashley said as she threw her arms around his neck, giving him a big hug. OK child what is all this commotion about? Wyoming the horse boldly asked in his deep voice? Ashley, I am so happy that you can talk to me. That sounds

Ashley's Story

like overkill Peter the Duck teasingly said. We can all talk.

Ashley, Peter has a lot of jokes he likes to tell and play on us. Well Peter, Wyoming said you better get all your jokes told before next month as it will be Thanksgiving. That is a time for thanking The Lord for all the blessings he has given us, not playing jokes on each other. Instinctively Peter the Duck swallowed hard as he put his wings together to pray. Ashley, giggled at Peter praying with one eye open and one eye closed.

I love you Wyoming Ashley excitedly repeated. You are my favorite horse ever. I love riding you and the time we spend together. I love our long rides in the mountains and I especially like it when we go in the fall to round up the cattle. Wyoming you are such a good horse. Ashley noticed Poocho was barking at the top of her lungs. Shh Poocho you are going to get us in trouble. Sweetie I don't think so

Ashley's Story

Speckles clucked, then added we all love you Ashley. I remember the time the Doctor told me I couldn't have chicks, Ashley you were by my side day and night. Stroking my feathers, trying to calm my fears.

Speckles turns to see her chicks nearing the stock tank. Get away from there, you might fall in and become fish bate. Speckles chicks ran towards her, crying out. At the same time Hattie, Peter and Wyoming busted out laughing

Judy Berg

and giggling. That's not right you are going to make those chicks sacred of water. Just isn't right Riff the turtle said in his low turtle voice. Well, Mr. know it all you get in the pond and be the life guard for my babies.

Ashley fell on her knees and hands laughing and giggling while Poocho was licking and jumping all over her.

Now Hattie look what you made that chicks do Speckles interjected. Come on Ashley

Ashley's Story

sweetheart get off your knees. Hattie can't help herself she is a comedian. No doubt, Wyoming said slightly giggling. I have to admit Wyoming does keep our spirts high said Hattie. I love y'all especially you Wyoming, as Ashley was getting up. Ashley was trying to stop Poocho from jumping up on her knocking her back down to the ground. Stop Poocho. Ashley gracefully walked up to Speckles asking may I hold one of your chicks? Do you know how to hold a

Judy Berg

chicken properly Speckles asked? Ashley replied yes. You gently but firmly grab with both hands. One hand over both wings, so they can't flap their wings. Have their beak facing out away from you, then gently tuck between your ribs and upper arm. Very good Speckles replied. Yes, you may hold one of my chicks. What is your name as Ashley gently picked up one of the baby chicks? Penelope said Hattie. Suddenly laughter and giggling penetrated the barn yard.

Ashley's Story

Meanwhile back at the house Papa and Gammie were sitting on the front porch, in their rocking chairs enjoying the cool afternoon. Sitting there watching the deer in the meadow, Gammie asked what are we going to do about Ashley? What do you mean Papa asked? Well you know your granddaughter just loves all animals, especially Wyoming. I know she comes home from school and can't wait to ride him. Her teacher says that is all she talks about at school is Wyoming.

Ashley, came running outside to the front porch, after her nap to tell Gammie Judy and Papa Ron about her dream. The animals were all talking she excitedly exclaimed!!! Slow down sweetheart you are talking so fast…..The animals they were all talking to me! Yes, dear, replied Gammie Judy. Papa asked Ashley were they talking that you could understand them? Yes, Papa every word. You know she gets

Ashley's Story

her passion for the animals from you, Papa responded, as he looked at Gammie Judy's house shoes with horse heads on them and her robe with cats and dogs all over it. Instinctively Papa shook his head as Ashley ran towards the barn. Spontaneously Gammie Judy and Papa Ron started giggling at the thought of the animals talking. We love our Ashley. She has such an imagination that child. I wonder where her God given gift for the love of animals will

Judy Berg

take her in this life? Gammie Judy and Papa Ron settled back in their rockers enjoying the late fall afternoon, admiring the fall colors orange, red and yellow knowing how blessed they truly are.

Ashley's Story

Judy Berg

Ashley's Story

Judy Berg

Ashley's Story

Judy Berg

www.ingramcontent.com/pod-product-compliance
Lightning Source LLC
Chambersburg PA
CBHW052127110526
44592CB00013B/1785